Those Who Wait

Biblical Stories for When God Seems Slow

Cover design by Macho Lara

Interior formatting by Microsoft Word

First edition, July 2025

www.macholara.com

DEDICATION

For the ones who are still waiting,
not for lack of faith,
but because faith keeps showing up
even when the answer doesn't.

*And for **Erica**,*
who has waited with me,
prayed beside me,
and believed even when I couldn't.

Table of Contents

INTRODUCTION

The Wait is Where We Live

Waiting is not a detour. It's not the blank space between real moments. It is where most of life unfolds...not after the prayer is answered, not once clarity arrives, not when the door finally opens, but here. In the uncertain middle.

We don't like this. We prefer arrival. We prefer progress. We like stories with climax and closure. But Scripture rarely gives us that kind of neat arc. More often, it offers tension that lingers, questions that stretch across generations, and promises that seem to take too long.

There's a reason for this. The Bible is not merely a record of events. It is the revelation of a God who forms people slowly, in real time, through real disappointment. It dares to show us what that looks like, not just when faith triumphs, but when it trembles.

The people of Scripture are not heroes because they always believed. They are examples because they kept walking even when belief was hard to come by.

This book is not about waiting for the sake of waiting. It's about what waiting does to us. And how, in God's hands, the process of waiting becomes more formative than the thing we're waiting for.

▪▪▪▪▪▪▪▪▪▪▪▪▪▪▪▪▪▪▪▪▪▪▪▪▪▪▪▪▪▪▪▪▪▪▪▪▪

A Pattern Across the Pages

From Genesis to the Gospels to Acts and beyond, waiting is not an exception. It's the pattern. Abraham and Sarah waiting for a child. Joseph waiting in prison. Hannah waiting in grief. David waiting for a throne. Mary waiting in mystery. The disciples waiting in prayer. Even Jesus Himself waits. He waits in the wilderness, in Gethsemane, and in the tomb.

These are not random delays. They are crucibles of transformation. And they invite us to pay attention to the kind of people we are becoming while we wait.

If your view of Scripture is shaped only by outcomes, you will likely miss its invitation. Waiting, in the biblical story, is not passive. It is participatory. It is the place where God invites trust, forms character, and teaches us to listen. That is what this book is about.

■■■■■■■■■■■■■■■■■■■■■■■■■■■■■■■■■■■■■■

Against the Grain of Easy Faith

A skeptical reader might ask: Why focus on waiting? Why not act? Why not move? Isn't faith about courage, action, momentum?

Yes. But biblically, action without waiting is often where trouble begins. Abraham sleeps with Hagar. Saul offers a sacrifice without Samuel. Peter draws a sword in Gethsemane. The impulse to act without listening, to fix without waiting, is deeply human and frequently harmful.

Waiting, in contrast, teaches restraint. Not as weakness, but as wisdom. It doesn't make you passive. It makes you rooted. And in a culture obsessed with speed, efficiency, and control, that's a different kind of strength.

■■■

What You'll Find Here

This book walks through the stories of six biblical moments of waiting:

- Abraham and Sarah – when the promise takes too long

- Joseph – when you're forgotten in the dark

- Hannah – when you feel forgotten by God

- David – when anointing doesn't mean arrival

- Mary – when the promise disrupts the present

- The disciples – when the Spirit tells you to stay still

Each story includes honest reflection, biblical exploration, and space to wrestle. There are no tidy conclusions or spiritual clichés here. There are only prayers for those who can barely pray, and space for those who are still trying to believe.

■■

A Word to the One Still Waiting

If you are holding a prayer that has not yet been answered, you are not alone.

If you are tired of simplistic advice, quick fixes, or faith that skips the hard parts, this book was written with you in mind.

And if you are somewhere between faith and doubt, between grief and hope, may these pages meet you in the tension. They won't give you easy answers. But perhaps they will offer companionship, reflection, and glimpses of the God who still speaks in the in-between.

■■■

How to Use This Book

This book can be read devotionally, studied alone, or explored in community. Each chapter ends with a **Reflection & Response** guide that is designed for group discussion, journaling, or quiet meditation.

If you are using this in a small group or discipleship setting, consider these rhythms:

- **Read the chapter before gathering**, slowly and reflectively.

- **Read the selected Scriptures together**, allowing time to pause and absorb them.

- **Engage the discussion prompts,** not to reach consensus but to hold space for honest wrestling.

- **Pray together**—even awkward, quiet, hesitant prayer is welcome.

- **Take the breath prayers or journaling sections into your week.**

The goal is not to finish a book. The goal is to learn how to wait well...with honesty, with hope, and with others. Let's begin.

CHAPTER 1 -

ABRAHAM & SARAH

▪▪▪▪▪▪▪▪▪▪▪▪▪▪▪▪▪▪▪▪▪▪▪▪▪▪▪▪▪▪▪▪▪▪▪▪▪▪

When the Promise Takes Too Long

Before God gives Abraham a son, He gives him a promise. Before Sarah laughs with joy, she laughs with disbelief. Between the first word from God and the sound of a baby's cry, twenty-five years pass. That is a long time to wait.

The promise is clear from the start. "I will make you into a great nation," God tells Abraham in Genesis 12:2. This is not vague encouragement. It is a direct call into a future Abraham did not ask for and could hardly comprehend.

But the years pass. They leave Ur. They settle in Canaan. They build altars. They survive a famine. They accumulate wealth and livestock and servants. They even rescue Lot from war. And still, no child.

Eventually, Abraham questions God. "What can You give me," he asks, "since I remain childless...?" (Genesis 15:2). God does not rebuke him. Instead, He reaffirms the promise. "Look up at the sky and count the stars... so shall your offspring be" (Genesis 15:5).

And still, nothing happens.

■■

The Weight of Delay

Waiting is not just the passage of time. It is the pressure of uncertainty. Abraham and Sarah are not passively sitting by. They are watching their bodies age. They are running out of options. They are doing the math. They are living with the ache.

This is where waiting begins to wound. When the gap between what God said and what we see starts to feel unbearable. When the voice of promise starts to sound like a memory, or worse, a mistake.

In Genesis 16, they act. Sarah gives Hagar, her Egyptian slave, to Abraham. This was a culturally acceptable practice, but it sidesteps the promise. Hagar conceives, and soon the household is in chaos. Jealousy, abuse, and abandonment follow. This is what happens when we try to force what only God can give.

But God is not finished with them. He does not revoke the promise. He reaffirms it again and again with more specificity. He changes Abram's name to Abraham, Sarai's to Sarah. He appears with angels. He says that by this time next year, Sarah will give birth.

And Sarah laughs.

It is not a joyful laugh. It is a skeptical, tired, protective laugh. "After I am worn out and my lord is old, will I now have this pleasure?" (Genesis 18:12). She has heard too much, hoped too long, and endured too many cycles of disappointment.

Her laughter is not rebellion. It is realism. It is the reflex of someone who has stopped trying to keep up appearances. And God hears it. But He does not punish her for it.

Instead, He replies with a question: "Is anything too hard for the Lord?" (Genesis 18:14).

That question is not just for Sarah. It is for every person who has grown tired of hoping. It is for those who dare to believe again, even when everything in them screams not to.

Exegetical Note: *Is anything too hard?*

The Hebrew phrase used here is *hā·yip̄·lē' mē·ʾăḏō·nāy.* literally, "Is anything too wonderful for the Lord?" The word translated "hard" (*yip̄lē'*) comes from the root *pala*, which means "to be extraordinary, surpassing, miraculous."

This is not a question of difficulty. It is a question of wonder. Of divine capacity. Of whether God still operates beyond the limits of human possibility.

It is also the first time in the Abraham narrative that God directly questions someone's reaction to the promise. It signals a turning point. Not just in the story, but in the soul.

■■■■■■■■■■■■■■■■■■■■■■■■■■■■■■■■■■■■■■■

Holding the Wait with Reverence

Isaac is born. The wait ends in joy. But the waiting itself was not wasted. Abraham and Sarah emerge as people who know God differently. Their relationship to the promise has changed. Their faith has been wrestled with. Their laughter has been redeemed.

But not everyone's story ends like theirs. That's what we must hold gently here. Many people wait and never see the outcome they longed for. Hebrews 11 even says this plainly: "These were all commended for their faith, yet none of them received what had been promised" (v. 39).

This does not make the waiting meaningless. It means the promise may be bigger than we can see. It stretches beyond us, sometimes even past our lifetime. But God remains faithful in the tension. His character holds when outcomes don't.

So what do we do with this story? We tell the truth. About how hard waiting can be. About how honest our doubts become. About how easily we try to take matters into our own hands. And how, even then, God keeps showing up.

Because maybe the real miracle isn't just that Sarah conceived. Maybe it's that she still believed. Maybe it's that she stayed. Maybe it's that her laughter, once protective and cynical, became joyful again.

That, too, is resurrection.

∎∎∎∎∎∎∎∎∎∎∎∎∎∎∎∎∎∎∎∎∎∎∎∎∎∎∎∎∎∎∎∎∎∎∎∎

Reflection & Response – Chapter 1

Abraham & Sarah – When the Promise Takes Too Long

Read Together

Genesis 12:1–5 – The initial call and promise

Genesis 15:1–6 – God's covenant and Abram's belief

Genesis 16:1–4, 15–16 – Sarah's plan and Hagar's son

Genesis 17:15–21 – God's reaffirmation of the promise

Genesis 18:1–15 – The divine visitors and Sarah's laugh

Genesis 21:1–7 – The birth of Isaac

■■■

Group Discussion Prompts

Use these open-ended prompts to guide conversation. Invite honesty and avoid rushing to resolve tension.

1. When have you felt like God's promises were taking too long?

Was it related to calling, healing, reconciliation, provision, or something else?

How did you react? Did your faith shrink, deepen, or feel suspended?

2. Abraham and Sarah devised their own plan when the wait became unbearable.

Have you ever "forced" a solution instead of trusting God's pace?

What does that teach you about fear, control, or longing?

3. Sarah laughed at God's promise — not a joyful laugh, but likely a weary one.

What kind of laughter do you bring to God these days: joyful, cynical, exhausted, or defiant?

Can laughter and faith coexist?

4. In Genesis 21, Sarah's laughter turns into joy.

What does it look like to let God rewrite your story in ways you couldn't script?

Is it harder to trust God's timing or God's goodness?

Personal Reflection & Journaling

Provide time for individuals to reflect quietly with pen and paper. Consider playing instrumental music or inviting silence for 5–10 minutes.

Reflect on these questions:

Where am I currently waiting on God, and what emotions am I carrying in that wait?

What fear or disappointment am I holding that's quietly shaping [or silencing] my prayers?

In what ways might God be shaping me during the delay, not just delivering something after it?

What would it look like to surrender the timeline but hold on to the promise?

Write a personal prayer that includes both your frustration and your faith.

■■■■■■■■■■■■■■■■■■■■■■■■■■■■■■■■■■■■■ ｜

A Practice of Trust (Optional Activity)

Breath Prayer

Introduce a simple prayer to carry into the week:

Inhale: *You are faithful…*

Exhale: *even in delay.*

Encourage group members to return to this breath prayer during moments of anxiety or restlessness.

■■■■■■■■■■■■■■■■■■■■■■■■■■■■■■■■■■■■■ ｜

Closing Prayer (Leader or Group)

*You may read this aloud or use it as a guide for a
shared prayer moment.*

Lord, like Abraham and Sarah, we confess
that we often grow weary in the waiting.
Our timelines run ahead of your Spirit. Our trust is
brittle.
But today we bring you our longings. We name
our disappointments.
And we ask that you would meet us in the middle
of the silence, not just at the end of it.
Help us to believe in your wonder, even when it
feels far off.
Teach us to wait, not with passivity, but with hope.
And when we laugh, let it become joy.

Amen.

Reflection Notes

Use this space to reflect on what God is stirring in

you...

CHAPTER 2 – JOSEPH

When You're Forgotten in the Dark

Some waits are lonely. Others feel like abandonment. Joseph knew both.

His story begins with favor. A multicolored robe. Dreams of greatness. A father who loves him more than his brothers can bear. He's seventeen. Confident. Naive. Chosen.

But the moment he shares his dreams, the unraveling begins.

He is thrown into a pit. Sold to traders. Taken to Egypt. Bought as property. Falsely accused. Imprisoned. Forgotten.

This is the shape of Joseph's waiting. Not passive stillness, but involuntary descent. Not the delay of a fulfilled plan, but the dismantling of everything he thought his life would be.

And it goes on for years.

■■■■■■■■■■■■■■■■■■■■■■■■■■■■■■■■■■■■■■■

The Descent

Genesis 37 to 40 covers the fall. Joseph's brothers strip him of his robe. They dip it in blood and lie to Jacob. Joseph, meanwhile, is dragged to Egypt and sold to Potiphar. There, he rises quickly in the household. Genesis 39:2 says, "The Lord was with Joseph and he prospered." But soon after, Potiphar's wife falsely accuses him of assault. And Joseph is thrown in prison.

What do you do when obedience leads to injustice?

What happens when doing the right thing only makes things worse?

The text offers no emotional window here. It doesn't say what Joseph thought or prayed. But we can imagine. Because we know what it is to feel forgotten. We know the silence that follows when we've tried to be faithful and still end up in the dark.

The Scriptures tell us that "the Lord was with Joseph" (Genesis 39:21). But the circumstances say otherwise. He is locked away. He has no defender. No advocate. No timeline.

And then, a flicker of hope.

■■ ı

The Cupbearer's Promise

While in prison, Joseph interprets dreams for Pharaoh's cupbearer and baker. The interpretations prove accurate. As the cupbearer is restored to his position, Joseph makes a simple request: "Remember me… show me kindness;

mention me to Pharaoh and get me out of this prison" (Genesis 40:14).

It's a deeply human moment. A plea for deliverance. A glimpse of self-advocacy in the midst of helplessness.

But the last verse of the chapter says it plainly: "The chief cupbearer, however, did not remember Joseph; he forgot him" (Genesis 40:23).

Two more years pass.

This part of Joseph's life is not just a side note in the narrative. It is the center. His transformation does not happen in the palace. It happens in the pit. In prison. In silence. In darkness.

■■

Waiting in the Dark

The Hebrew word for "pit" in Genesis 37:24 is bôr. often used for cisterns, wells, or empty holding spaces. Metaphorically, it becomes a symbol of death, isolation, or abandonment throughout the Hebrew Scriptures.

David later cries out, "He lifted me out of the slimy pit... out of the mud and mire" (Psalm 40:2). Jeremiah is literally thrown into one (Jeremiah 38). For Joseph, the pit is both literal and spiritual. It is the container of disappointment. The womb of transformation.

Waiting in the pit strips you. Of illusions. Of control. Of the story you thought your life was going to tell.

But in the darkness, something else can be born. Humility. Dependence. Clarity. A different kind of strength. A quieter kind of faith.

We are told that God was with Joseph. But this presence does not always remove the pain. It does not always shorten the wait. It does not always bring justice on our schedule.

It does, however, mean the pit is not the end of the story.

■■■■■■■■■■■■■■■■■■■■■■■■■■■■■■■■■■■■■■

Resurrection by Way of Obscurity

Joseph's rise comes suddenly. Pharaoh has dreams no one can interpret. The cupbearer remembers. Joseph is summoned. Cleaned. Clothed. And within hours, he is made second-in-command of all Egypt.

But his rise is not the climax. It is the fruit of what was formed in the pit. Joseph governs with wisdom because he knows what it's like to be powerless. He forgives his brothers because he remembers what betrayal feels like. He preserves life because he has learned the weight of loss.

And yet, even as he sees God's hand in all of it, there are signs the wounds remain. When his first son is born, he names him Manasseh, saying, "It is because God has made me forget all my trouble and all my father's household" (Genesis 41:51). Forgetting, here, is not literal erasure. It is survival. It is a way of saying, "I've had to make peace with pain I will never fully make sense of."

∎∎∎∎∎∎∎∎∎∎∎∎∎∎∎∎∎∎∎∎∎∎∎∎∎∎∎∎∎∎∎∎∎∎∎∎∎

Let the Pit Speak

Not every pit ends with a promotion. Not every dark season resolves with vindication. Sometimes you are forgotten and remain there longer than you can bear.

But Joseph's story reminds us that the dark is not wasted. And that God's presence is not proven by speed, but by faithfulness in silence.

You may not see the arc of your story yet. You may not be able to name the purpose. But the God who was with Joseph is still with you. And in time, the pit may become the place where your soul was formed.

■■■

Reflection & Response – Chapter 2

Joseph – When You're Forgotten in the Dark

Read Together

Genesis 37:1–28 – Joseph's dreams and betrayal

Genesis 39 – Joseph's integrity and imprisonment

Genesis 40 – Forgotten by the cupbearer

Genesis 41:1–16 – Remembered at the right time

Genesis 50:15–21 – Joseph's forgiveness and perspective

■■■■■■■■■■■■■■■■■■■■■■■■■■■■■■■■■■■■■■

Group Discussion Prompts

Use these prompts to foster honest, spacious conversation. Let the tension linger when needed — Joseph's story unfolds slowly.

1. Have you ever been overlooked or forgotten?

Whether by people, systems, or even God — what did that experience stir up in you?

What helped you endure it, or what made it harder?

2. Joseph remained faithful in a place where no one saw him.

What does faithfulness look like when no one is applauding, affirming, or promoting you?

Can obedience in obscurity still carry purpose?

3. How do you hold on to integrity in unjust situations?

Joseph refused to compromise, even when it cost him.

Have you faced a similar decision? What values kept you anchored?

4. In Genesis 50:20, Joseph says, "You intended to harm me, but God intended it for good."

How do you honestly process harm and healing without minimizing either one?

Is there something in your life you've begun to see differently, in hindsight?

∎∎

Personal Reflection & Journaling

Allow time for individuals to sit quietly with these questions. Encourage honest reflection, even if it feels unfinished.

Reflect on these questions:

Where in my life do I feel "imprisoned" —
stuck, unseen, or misunderstood?

Who or what have I been waiting on to
remember me?

Have I been tempted to give up on
faithfulness in the dark?

What do I believe God is forming in me that I
can't yet see?

**Write a prayer naming your desire to be
seen and remembered — by God and by
others — without needing to rush the process.**

■■■■■■■■■■■■■■■■■■■■■■■■■■■■■■■■■■■■■ ■■ ı

A Practice of Presence (Optional Activity)

Silence with Intention

Invite the group into two minutes of shared
silence. Set a timer. Ask them to sit with the
phrase:

"God is near, even here."

Afterward, let them share how the silence felt —
comforting, awkward, resistant — without
judgment.

■■■

Closing Prayer (Leader or Group)

*Read slowly or adapt as needed. Let it become
communal or contemplative.*

God of the forgotten, You see us even when
others don't.

You remember us when it feels like no one else
does.

We confess the ways we've questioned your
presence,

Not because we lack faith, but because the dark
sometimes feels too long.

Shape in us the kind of trust that does not
vanish in the shadows.

Make our faith resilient — not performative.

Teach us to wait, like Joseph, with open hands and upright hearts,

And remind us that you are never absent, only quiet.

In the silence, let us be formed.

Amen.

Reflection Notes

Use this space to reflect on what God is stirring in

you...

CHAPTER 3 - HANNAH

When You Feel Forgotten by God

Hannah is not the first woman in Scripture to wait for a child, but her story brings that ache into full emotional clarity. Unlike Sarah, she has no divine visitor. Unlike Rebekah or Rachel, she has no father or husband pleading on her behalf. Hannah is alone, year after year, voiceless in her sorrow, visible only in her pain.

Her story opens not with hope, but with heartbreak. First Samuel 1 tells us that "the Lord had closed her womb." Those are hard words. They name a kind of divine agency that feels painful, even offensive. But they are not the end of the story.

■■■■■■■■■■■■■■■■■■■■■■■■■■■■■■■■■■■■■■

A Wound That Is Seen by Others

Hannah is one of two wives. Elkanah, her husband, gives her "a double portion" because he loves her, but "the Lord had closed her womb" (1 Samuel 1:5). The other wife, Peninnah, has children. She provokes Hannah "to irritate her" (v. 6). Every year, during their pilgrimage to Shiloh, this dynamic erupts.

There is a brutal line in the text: "This went on year after year" (v. 7). Waiting is one thing. Waiting in the presence of shame is another.

Hannah weeps. She does not eat. Elkanah, well-meaning but clueless, asks, "Why are you weeping? Don't I mean more to you than ten sons?" (v. 8). This is not comfort. It is deflection. Her pain is misunderstood. Her longing is minimized. And still, she prays.

■■

The Bitter Prayer

One year, Hannah enters the house of the Lord and prays with a different kind of desperation. The Hebrew says she is "deeply troubled" (*marat nefesh*. literally "bitter of soul"), and she weeps "much and prayed to the Lord" (v. 10).

She makes a vow: "Lord Almighty, if You will... remember me and not forget Your servant... then I will give him to the Lord for all the days of his life" (v. 11).

This prayer is not transactional. It is covenantal. She is not bargaining. She is entrusting. The phrase "remember me" is deeply significant. It echoes the prayers of others in distress. like Samson (Judges 16:28) and Nehemiah (Nehemiah 13:14). To ask God to remember is to say, "See

me. Acknowledge me. Act according to Your
mercy."

■■■ ı

Misunderstood in Worship

Eli the priest sees her. But instead of
recognizing her devotion, he assumes she is drunk.
He rebukes her: "How long are you going to stay
drunk? Put away your wine" (v. 14).

This is insult added to injury. She is judged
by the very place that should have offered
sanctuary. But Hannah speaks with bold clarity: "I
am a woman who is deeply troubled... I have been
praying here out of my great anguish and grief"
(vv. 15–16).

Eli, to his credit, realizes his mistake and
blesses her. "Go in peace, and may the God of
Israel grant you what you have asked of Him" (v.
17).

Something shifts in Hannah. "Her face was no longer downcast" (v. 18). The text does not say she is pregnant. Only that her countenance has changed. Her soul is steadied. Her anguish has been heard.

■■■■■■■■■■■■■■■■■■■■■■■■■■■■■■■■■■■■■■■

From Waiting to Worship

Hannah conceives. She names the child Samuel, saying, "Because I asked the Lord for him" (v. 20). But what happens next is perhaps the most remarkable part of her story.

She keeps her vow.

When the child is weaned, she brings him to the temple and offers him to the Lord. "I prayed for this child," she says, "and the Lord has granted me what I asked of Him. So now I give him to the Lord" (vv. 27–28).

This is not the resolution of her waiting. It is the transformation of her faith.

She does not just receive the gift. She releases it. And in doing so, she becomes a model of what it means to hold even our answered prayers with open hands.

■■■■■■■■■■■■■■■■■■■■■■■■■■■■■■■■■■■■■■■

The Song That Follows

Chapter 2 opens with Hannah's prayer. a poetic, prophetic song that rivals the Psalms in its depth. "My heart rejoices in the Lord... there is no one holy like the Lord; there is no one besides You" (1 Samuel 2:1–2).

She proclaims that the barren woman has borne children, that the poor are raised, that the lowly are lifted. Her song prefigures Mary's Magnificat in Luke 1. It is the voice of one who has been heard by God and now declares that God hears the lowly.

Hannah's story does not promise us that all longings will be met. But it shows us what it means to bring them, honestly and persistently, into the presence of God. Her waiting is not passive. It is worshipful. It is embodied faith.

. . . .

Faith in the Tension

What if Hannah had never conceived? Would her prayer still matter? Would God still be good?

These are the hard questions we must sit with. Because some people pray like Hannah and never get what they asked for. Some carry sorrow to the grave.

But Hannah's story, at its core, is not just about getting what she wanted. It is about a soul that dares to bring its bitterness to God. It is about waiting that leads to worship. It is about being seen, even before being answered.

And that is something all of us can cling to.

■■

Reflection & Response – Chapter 3

Hannah – When You Feel Forgotten by God

Read Together

1 Samuel 1:1–18 – Hannah's grief and prayer

1 Samuel 1:19–28 – God's response and Hannah's faithfulness

1 Samuel 2:1–10 – Hannah's song of praise

■■

Group Discussion Prompts

These prompts are meant to help participants hold grief, longing, and faith in the same breath — just as Hannah did.

1. Hannah was deeply distressed and poured out her soul to God.

When have you prayed from a place of honest

anguish or raw longing?

How did God respond — or not respond — in that season?

2. Hannah was misunderstood by Eli, the priest, who mistook her prayer for drunkenness.

Have you ever felt misjudged in your spiritual struggle?

What does it feel like when your pain is dismissed or misread by others — especially in the Church?

3. After praying, Scripture says Hannah's face was no longer downcast — even before she became pregnant.

What shifted in Hannah? What does it mean to walk away from prayer with peace, even when nothing has changed yet?

4. Hannah's song in chapter 2 is bold and worshipful — a theology shaped by pain.

How has your understanding of God been shaped by seasons of unanswered prayers?

Is it possible to worship while still wondering why?

▪▪▪

Personal Reflection & Journaling

Offer a quiet space for inward reflection. Invite honesty without pressure to resolve tension.

Reflect on these questions:

Where in my life do I feel forgotten, overlooked, or unseen by God?

What unspoken desires have I buried instead of bringing to God?

How do I respond when others misunderstand my pain or minimize my story?

What would it look like to bring my grief to God without guarding or sanitizing it?

**Write a personal prayer like Hannah's —
one that holds your sorrow and longing in the
presence of God.**

▪▪▪▪▪▪▪▪▪▪▪▪▪▪▪▪▪▪▪▪▪▪▪▪▪▪▪▪▪▪▪▪▪▪▪▪▪

A Practice of Honesty (Optional Activity)

Lament in Community

Encourage each person to write a one- or two-sentence lament using this structure:

"Lord, I feel _____ because _____, but I trust you are still _____."

Invite those who feel comfortable to share theirs aloud. Create space to honor what is spoken without trying to fix or explain.

▪▪▪▪▪▪▪▪▪▪▪▪▪▪▪▪▪▪▪▪▪▪▪▪▪▪▪▪▪▪▪▪▪▪▪▪▪

Closing Prayer (Leader or Group)

You may read or pray this as written or allow participants to add lines of their own lament or hope.

God who hears the unheard,
We bring to you our private ache and our silent prayers,
And the questions we've stopped asking out loud.

Like Hannah, we bring our weeping and our waiting.
We trust that you collect every tear, that you see past the surface,
And that you are present — even when your voice is quiet.

Form in us a hope that doesn't erase grief.
Give us the courage to pray again.
And teach us to believe that you are still writing stories of redemption,

Even when our page feels blank.

Amen.

Reflection Notes

Use this space to reflect on what God is stirring in

you...

CHAPTER 4 - DAVID

When Anointing Doesn't Mean Arrival

The prophet Samuel comes to Jesse's house looking for a king. God has rejected Saul, and He tells Samuel that the next king will come from among Jesse's sons. One by one, the older brothers pass before him, tall and impressive. But God says no.

Then David is brought in from the fields. He is young. Ruddy. Smelling of sheep. And God says, "Rise and anoint him; this is the one" (1 Samuel 16:12).

David is chosen. He is anointed with oil in the presence of his family. The Spirit of the Lord comes upon him in power.

And then, he goes back to tending sheep.

This is the beginning of David's wait.

■■

Called but Not Crowned

There is a dangerous myth in Christian culture that calling should lead directly to promotion. But David's life dismantles that idea. He is chosen by God but rejected by the world. He has the Spirit, but not the scepter. The throne has his name on it, but Saul is still sitting in it.

What do you do when you are anointed for something but not yet appointed to it?

David waits. But not passively. He plays music in Saul's court. He defeats Goliath. He leads armies. He gains the favor of the people. And Saul grows jealous.

From that point on, David's life becomes a fugitive's story. He hides in caves. He dodges spears. He loses his mentor Samuel. He watches friends die. He pretends to be insane in foreign cities. He gathers a ragtag group of misfits in the wilderness. He writes psalms in hiding.

The anointing is not protection from hardship. It is, in some ways, a path into it.

■■■■■■■■■■■■■■■■■■■■■■■■■■■■■■■■■■■■■■

The Wilderness as Seminary

David's years on the run are not wasted. They are formative. The wilderness becomes a kind of seminary, a crucible where character is shaped.

In 1 Samuel 24, David finds Saul in a vulnerable position inside a cave. His men whisper, "This is the day the Lord spoke of… take his life." But David refuses. "The Lord forbid that I should do such a thing to my master, the Lord's anointed" (v. 6).

This is restraint formed by reverence. David does not grasp what God has not yet given. He honors a man who has tried to kill him. He chooses the long road.

Again in chapter 26, David has another opportunity to kill Saul while he sleeps. Again he refuses. He takes Saul's spear and water jug, proves his innocence, and calls from a distance.

These moments show a heart shaped not just by calling but by submission. David knows he has been chosen, but he refuses to force the timing. He lets God be God.

Between the Anointing and the Crown

The gap between promise and fulfillment is often longer than we expect. David lives in that gap for years. Scholars estimate it may have been fifteen to twenty years between his anointing and his coronation.

During that time, he experiences loss, betrayal, fear, and exhaustion. He loses Jonathan, his closest friend. He feigns loyalty to foreign kings. He makes terrible decisions. But he also seeks God. He writes poetry. He asks for guidance. He keeps returning to the Lord.

This kind of waiting tests the soul. It confronts every impulse toward self-promotion. It exposes the difference between charisma and character. And it asks one haunting question: Will you still trust God when His timing humiliates you?

David could have taken the shortcut. He could have claimed what was rightfully his. But he chose something harder. He chose to believe that what God begins, God must finish. Not in David's time. In God's.

■■■■■■■■■■■■■■■■■■■■■■■■■■■■■■■■■■■■■■■

Exegetical Note: *"I will not lift my hand..."*

In both 1 Samuel 24:6 and 26:11, David repeats the phrase, "I will not lift my hand against the Lord's anointed." The Hebrew verb used here, *šālaḥ*, means "to send forth" or "stretch out." It is an active verb of intent. David is not just refusing to harm Saul; he is restraining his power.

This restraint is not fear. It is reverence. David understands that if he takes the throne by force, he undermines the very calling God placed on his life. He refuses to become the kind of king Saul was.

The wilderness tests whether David will become the kind of leader worth following. His decisions in obscurity are shaping his capacity for authority.

■■■

What the Anointing Doesn't Guarantee

Being called does not guarantee ease. Being gifted does not guarantee opportunity. Being faithful does not guarantee quick results.

David's story reminds us that waiting does not invalidate the anointing. Delayed arrival is not the same as divine rejection. Sometimes the crown comes slow. Not because God has forgotten, but because God is forming something deeper.

You may be living in that in-between space. You may feel like you've been called to something that has yet to materialize. The temptation to force the outcome will always be near. But the story of David whispers: Wait. Don't grasp what God hasn't given.

The wilderness is not your end. But it might be your training ground.

■■■■■■■■■■■■■■■■■■■■■■■■■■■■■■■■■■■■■■■

Reflection & Response – Chapter 4

David – When Anointing Doesn't Mean Arrival

Read Together

1 Samuel 16:1–13 – David anointed as king

1 Samuel 17:12–37 – David's obscurity and courage

1 Samuel 18:5–16 – Saul's jealousy and David's rejection

1 Samuel 24 – David spares Saul

2 Samuel 2:1–4; 5:1–5 – David finally becomes king

■■■

Group Discussion Prompts

Use these prompts to explore the tension between calling and timing, anointing and arrival.

1. David was anointed long before he was appointed.

Have you ever sensed God's calling in your life but had to wait a long time to see it realized?

How do you handle the space between the promise and the platform?

2. Even after being anointed, David returned to tending sheep.

What does it mean to be faithful in small things when you've been called to more?

Can you serve in obscurity without resenting it?

3. David had opportunities to "take" what God had promised (like killing Saul), but he chose restraint.

Have you ever been tempted to force something that God may eventually provide in His timing?

What helps you trust God's pace when shortcuts look appealing?

4. David spent years fleeing and hiding, despite being chosen.

What do you think God was forming in him during that long, slow journey?

What has God formed in you during delayed seasons?

■■■■■■■■■■■■■■■■■■■■■■■■■■■■■■■■■■■■■■■

Personal Reflection & Journaling

Give space for participants to reflect quietly, with openness to both frustration and faith.

Reflect on these questions:

Where have I sensed God's anointing but not yet seen the fulfillment?

Have I been tempted to rush ahead of God's timing or prove my calling to others?

What does faithful presence look like in the "in-between" seasons of life?

In what ways is God developing character in me before giving clarity or promotion?

Write a personal prayer like Hannah's — one that holds your sorrow and longing in the presence of God.

■■■■■■■■■■■■■■■■■■■■■■■■■■■■■■■■■■■■■■

A Practice of Honesty (Optional Activity)

Lament in Community

Encourage each person to write a one- or two-sentence lament using this structure:

"Lord, I feel _____ because _____, but I trust you are still _____."

Invite those who feel comfortable to share theirs aloud. Create space to honor what is spoken without trying to fix or explain.

■■■■■■■■■■■■■■■■■■■■■■■■■■■■■■■■■■■■■■

Closing Prayer (Leader or Group)

You may read or pray this as written, or invite the group to add lines about their own callings and delays.

God who anoints before we arrive, You see what no one else sees.
You name purpose before others affirm it. And still, your timing humbles us.

When we are misunderstood, remind us that you know our name.
When we are overlooked, remind us that Your calling still stands.
When the path is not a straight line, give us the patience to walk with you, not ahead of you.

Teach us to trust your preparation in the unseen places and to serve without recognition.
Teach us to wait without bitterness, and to worship in the wilderness.

You formed David in caves and quiet fields
— form us there too.

And when the time is right,
Help us to step forward not with pride,
But with faith refined by waiting.

Amen.

Reflection Notes

Use this space to reflect on what God is stirring in

you…

CHAPTER 5 - MARY

When the Promise Disrupts the Present

Mary wasn't planning for an angel.

She wasn't preparing for the divine to show up in her neighborhood, let alone her body. She was engaged to Joseph, likely in her early teens, perhaps living with quiet dreams about married life, stability, and a modest home in Nazareth. Nothing in her story made her seem like the kind of person God would pick for anything remarkable.

But Gabriel arrived with a disruptive word: she was favored, and she would carry a promise that would reshape the world.

"You will conceive and give birth to a son, and you are to call him Jesus. He will be great and will be called the

Son of the Most High."
(Luke 1:31–32)

That promise was not only holy. It was unsettling. It meant risk, rejection, and a story she could not control. Mary did not argue, but neither did she pretend the road would be easy. Her question wasn't defiant. It was honest: *"How can this be?"*

Even in her confusion, she responded not with protest, but surrender:

"I am the Lord's servant… May your word to me be fulfilled."
(Luke 1:38)

She accepted the call before she understood the cost.
She embraced the promise before it was proven.
She yielded her plans without a timeline.

This is where waiting begins for Mary. Not in silence or exile, like others in Scripture, but in disruption. The promise doesn't come when life is barren, but when life seems predictable. And it doesn't merely delay her future. It disrupts her present.

■■■■■■■■■■■■■■■■■■■■■■■■■■■■■■■■■■■■■■

Mary's Surrender Is Not Shallow

Too often we romanticize Mary's obedience. We treat it like a clean, joyful moment of blind faith. But her surrender wasn't passive. It was active, deliberate, and deeply courageous. To say yes meant trusting God with her reputation, her relationships, and her body. She bore a promise no one would believe and shouldered the weight of shame that came with it.

And yet, when she visits Elizabeth (another woman marked by miraculous conception) Mary begins to sing.

Her song, often called the *Magnificat*, is not a lullaby. It is a declaration. A vision of reversal. A proclamation of a God who brings down the powerful and lifts the lowly. She interprets her disruption as part of God's bigger story, and that gives her voice strength:

"My soul glorifies the Lord
and my spirit rejoices in God my Savior..."
(Luke 1:46–47)

She praises God not because everything is clear, but because God is faithful. The disruption has not been resolved, but it has been reframed.

■■

The Disruption Continues

Even after the birth of Jesus, the promise continues to disrupt Mary's life. She gives birth in a strange town, among animals, with no proper place to stay. Her son is worshiped by shepherds and prophesied over by strangers, but he is still a baby...fragile and dependent. She is told a sword will pierce her soul (Luke 2:35), and she stores all of this in her heart, not knowing what it will mean.

The waiting doesn't end with Jesus' arrival. It only deepens.

She still must raise him, protect him, lose him in the temple, follow him through ministry, watch him suffer, and eventually stand at the foot of the cross. Her "yes" to God led her through joy, but also through loss.

And this is often the case with us. The promise of God doesn't always bring immediate peace. Sometimes, it turns our world upside down. It disorients us, removes our safety nets, and asks for faith we didn't know we had.

Mary shows us that waiting isn't always about the future. Sometimes, it's about letting the present be interrupted. It's about carrying something that feels too big for us, but still choosing to say: *Let it be.*

■■■■■■■■■■■■■■■■■■■■■■■■■■■■■■■■■■■■■■■

When God's Promise Finds You

You don't have to understand everything to obey.

You don't have to feel ready to be chosen.

You don't have to see the full picture to sing.

Mary's story invites us to trust God not only when life feels empty, but when it feels full and settled. Because sometimes, God's promise won't simply fill the gaps. It will dismantle the plans. It will ask for more than you expected, but offer more than you imagined.

And in the midst of that disruption, faith can still grow.

Sometimes the holiest thing you can do is simply say,

"I'm listening. I'm open. Let it be."

▪▪▪▪▪▪▪▪▪▪▪▪▪▪▪▪▪▪▪▪▪▪▪▪▪▪▪▪▪▪▪▪▪▪▪▪▪▪

Reflection & Response – Chapter 5

Mary – When the Promise Disrupts the Present

Read Together

Luke 1:26–38 – The angel's announcement

Luke 1:39–56 – Mary visits Elizabeth and sings her song

Matthew 1:18–25 – Joseph's response to the news

Luke 2:1–7 – The birth of Jesus in Bethlehem

▪▪▪▪▪▪▪▪▪▪▪▪▪▪▪▪▪▪▪▪▪▪▪▪▪▪▪▪▪▪▪▪▪▪▪▪▪▪

Group Discussion Prompts

Use these to explore how unexpected, holy disruptions shape our obedience.

1. Mary's "yes" came at a great cost.

Have you ever sensed God asking something of you that disrupted your expectations, reputation, or plans?

What was your honest response?

2. Mary's surrender was immediate, but not shallow.

She didn't demand answers or guarantees — only clarity about what God was asking.

What does it look like to say "yes" without knowing what's next?

3. The promise she received brought scandal and misunderstanding.

Has obedience to God ever created tension with others around you?

How do you respond when faithfulness leads to misunderstanding or rejection?

4. Mary visited Elizabeth, and her burden turned into a song.

Who do you go to when your faith needs strengthening?

How can community give voice to what feels uncertain or overwhelming?

■■■■■■■■■■■■■■■■■■■■■■■■■■■■■■■■■■■■■

Personal Reflection & Journaling

Create quiet space for participants to process these prompts through journaling or silence.

Reflect on these questions:

Where in my life is God asking for a costly "yes"?

Am I willing to obey without full understanding or approval?

What promise has disrupted my expectations of how life would go?

What would it mean to carry that promise with worship rather than worry?

Write a personal prayer like Hannah's — one that holds your sorrow and longing in the presence of God.

■■■■■■■■■■■■■■■■■■■■■■■■■■■■■■■■■■■■■■■

A Practice of Surrender (Optional Activity)

Open-Hands Posture Prayer

Invite group members to sit with their hands open on their lap, palms facing up.

Instruct them to name silently what they are releasing to God, and what promise or calling they are open to receiving.

End by praying together:

"Lord, not as I will, but as you will. Help me to hold nothing too tightly."

■■■■■■■■■■■■■■■■■■■■■■■■■■■■■■■■■■■■■

Closing Prayer (Leader or Group)

You can read this aloud or allow group members to speak out phrases of surrender together.

God who speaks into ordinary rooms and asks extraordinary things,
You do not always come when it's convenient,
You do not always explain,
But you always invite.

Like Mary, may we respond with wonder instead of control.
May we open ourselves to what you are birthing in our lives.
Even if it's hard. Even if it costs us. Even if no one else understands.

Help us carry your promise, not with fear, but with faith.
And when it disrupts our plans, let it also deepen

our praise.

Amen.

Reflection Notes

Use this space to reflect on what God is stirring in

you...

CHAPTER 6 –

THE DISCIPLES

When the Spirit Tells You to Stay Still

"Do not leave Jerusalem, but wait for the gift my Father promised…".Acts 1:4

They had seen everything. The betrayal. The trial. The cross. The stone rolled back. The scarred hands. The risen Jesus, standing in front of them, teaching again.

Their grief had been interrupted by resurrection. Their fear was replaced with astonishment. Their purpose was restored.

It would have been reasonable to assume this was the moment to go. After all, Jesus had spoken of making disciples, of bearing witness to the ends of the earth. The world was broken. The people were waiting. The truth was burning in their hearts.

But the very next words Jesus gives them are not "Go." They are "Wait."

"Do not leave Jerusalem. Wait for the gift my Father promised." (Acts 1:4)

Not move. Not act. Not build. Wait.

■■■■■■■■■■■■■■■■■■■■■■■■■■■■■■■■■■■■■■■

A Command that Feels Like Delay

The instruction in Acts 1 is not vague. The Greek verb used, *perimenō*,.means to remain, to abide expectantly, to stay near. It carries both proximity and patience. Jesus is not telling them to go back to life as usual. He is telling them to stay still in a posture of expectancy.

This is not a moment of weakness. It is a command of preparation. The resurrection did not mark the end of waiting. It introduced a new kind.

They are living between appearances. Jesus is alive, but soon He will ascend. The Holy Spirit is promised but not yet poured out. Their calling is real, but the equipping is not yet complete.

They must sit in the uncertainty between revelation and empowerment. Their only job is to wait.

For many of us, that's the hardest part of faith.

We are conditioned to act, to solve, to build, to initiate. We equate movement with faithfulness. But here, Jesus equates faithfulness with stillness.

He is saying: Don't do anything until the Spirit arrives.

That requires trust. It also requires restraint.

Together in the Upper Room

After Jesus ascends, the disciples do exactly what He said. They return to the upper room in Jerusalem—a place marked by memory. It's where they shared the Last Supper. Where confusion and failure once took hold. Now, it becomes the space of gathered obedience.

Luke tells us they "joined together constantly in prayer" (Acts 1:14). This was not idle waiting. It was alert, collective dependence. Men and women. Mary, the mother of Jesus. The apostles. Other followers. All staying still, together, trusting that something was coming, even if they didn't know what it would be.

There is no sign that they knew how long it would take. No timeline. No reassurance. No blueprint.

They waited in community. They waited in worship. They waited in the absence of certainty.

■■■■■■■■■■■■■■■■■■■■■■■■■■■■■■■■■■■■■■■

What Waiting Reveals

It is worth noting that Pentecost does not come because they earned it. It does not arrive as the result of their perfect prayers, or their emotional intensity, or their spiritual fervor.

The Spirit comes because God promised it would.

The Spirit comes in grace and power, on a timeline not of their choosing. And when it does, it changes everything.

Tongues of fire. A rushing wind. Boldness they had not mustered on their own. Clarity they could not conjure. Words they did not rehearse.

But the power of Pentecost did not begin with the wind. It began with the waiting.

That waiting created unity. It exposed their need. It reminded them they were not in control of the timeline, the method, or the outcome.

They were told to wait, and they did.

And when the Spirit moved, they moved with Him.

■■■■■■■■■■■■■■■■■■■■■■■■■■■■■■■■■■■■■■■

The Spirit Still Tells Us to Wait

We want to be effective. We want to be faithful. We want to fulfill our calling. But sometimes, obedience means sitting still until the next instruction comes.

We are not often taught how to do this. Even in ministry, we are taught to lead, to initiate, to push forward. But if the first act of the Church was to wait, then surely this is part of our formation too.

There are times when the Spirit says, "Not yet." When the right thing would become the wrong thing if done out of season. When launching prematurely could do more harm than good.

Learning to discern this is a mark of spiritual maturity.

The question is not just What is God calling me to do? It is also Is now the time?

The disciples show us that trust is not proven by motion, but by submission. They did not create revival. They created space for it.

We are not the initiators of power. We are the vessels. And waiting is how God gets us ready.

▪▪

Reflection & Response – Chapter 6

The Disciples – When the Spirit Tells You to Stay Still

Read Together

Luke 24:36–53 – Jesus' final appearance and instructions

Acts 1:1–11 – The command to wait for the Holy Spirit

Acts 1:12–14 – The disciples gather and pray

Acts 2:1–4 – The arrival of the Holy Spirit

■■■■■■■■■■■■■■■■■■■■■■■■■■■■■■■■■■■■■■■

Group Discussion Prompts

Use these prompts to explore the unique challenge of obedient stillness.

1. Jesus told the disciples to wait — not to act.

How does it feel when you sense God calling you to wait, even when you're ready to move?

Why do you think stillness is often harder than action?

2. They waited in a room together.

What's the value of waiting in community rather than isolation?

Are there people in your life who help you wait well?

3. The Holy Spirit came suddenly, but not randomly.

What does it mean to trust that God's timing isn't late, even when it feels delayed?

Have you ever experienced a breakthrough or clarity that came after a long wait?

4. The disciples didn't know what the Holy Spirit's arrival would look like — only that it would happen.

What unknowns are you holding before God?

Can you remain faithful even when the outcome is unclear?

■■■■■■■■■■■■■■■■■■■■■■■■■■■■■■■■■■■■■

Personal Reflection & Journaling

Invite participants to enter a posture of quiet attentiveness.

Reflect on these questions:

Where do I feel the tension between wanting to act and being called to wait?

What emotions arise when I feel inactive — anxiety, guilt, fear, relief?

Who has God placed around me to wait with? Have I been willing to receive their presence?

What might the Holy Spirit be preparing in me as I sit still before God?

Write a prayer of readiness. Not readiness to move, but readiness to receive.

■■■■■■■■■■■■■■■■■■■■■■■■■■■■■■■■■■■■■■■

A Practice of Stillness (Optional Activity)

Silent Listening Prayer

Guide the group into 5 minutes of complete silence.

Before beginning, invite them to repeat this simple prayer internally:

> *"Speak, Lord — your servant is listening."*

After the silence, allow optional space for people to share if they sensed anything — a word, phrase, image, or feeling.

■■

Closing Prayer (Leader or Group)

This prayer is written slowly, inviting a meditative pace. You may speak it together or responsively.

Holy Spirit, You do not rush.

You are not hurried by our fear or our frustration.

You do not need our performance.

You invite our presence.

Teach us to stay, to listen, to pray in the upper
rooms of our lives,

Even when the world outside tells us to move, to
do, to prove.

Remind us that waiting is not wasted.

That silence is not abandonment.

And that the wind of your presence will come,

even if we do not know when.

Give us courage to wait.

And joy when your fire falls.

Amen.

Reflection Notes

Use this space to reflect on what God is stirring in

you…

EPILOGUE

The Story God is Still Writing

Waiting is not just a theme in Scripture. It is the shape of the story itself.

Abraham waits. Joseph waits. Israel waits. David waits. Mary waits. The early Church waits. And even now, we wait. Not passively. Not aimlessly. But with hearts that are still learning to trust.

These are not just ancient stories. They are mirrors. They remind us that even the faithful struggle. That those who are called are not always quick to understand. That promises are sometimes held longer than we thought our hands could carry them.

Scripture does not gloss over this tension. It does not pretend that waiting is easy. It shows the cracks. It names the tears. It records the questions. And somehow, it still invites us to hope.

Hope is not a denial of reality. It is the decision to anchor ourselves in something deeper. Not in outcomes or timelines, but in the character of God. In His presence with us, even when the path disappears from view.

The Church itself is shaped by this rhythm. Every generation has learned to live between promise and fulfillment. Between resurrection and return. We celebrate what Christ has done, even as we cry out for what He has not yet completed. That cry is not a lack of faith. It is the sound of faith still breathing.

If you are in a season of waiting, you are not failing. You are not forgotten. You are standing in a sacred tradition. You are walking a road others have walked before you. And every step you take, no matter how faltering, is seen.

Your waiting may never get a headline. It may not resolve how you hope. But it is still part of the story God is telling. A story not of perfect outcomes, but of people who keep showing up. People who pray, even when their voice shakes. People who stay, even when they do not understand. People who trust, even when they are not sure what tomorrow holds.

So do not rush past this. Do not despise the in-between. The God who met Abraham under the stars, who sat with Joseph in a prison cell, who listened to Hannah's whispered grief, who found David in the cave, who overshadowed Mary with promise…this same God is with you.

And He is still writing.

A Prayer for the One Still Waiting

God of the slow and sacred path,

You do not rush what You love.

You are never hurried, yet never absent.

You are near in the quiet,

present in the questions,

and faithful even when the road is long.

We confess that we grow tired in the waiting.

We confess that our hope wears thin.

But You are still the God who waits with us.

So teach us to wait in ways that shape us,

to trust You with what we cannot control,

to walk forward with hearts still open.

Like Abraham and Sarah,

teach us to trust when the promise takes too long.

When the years stretch on and our hope feels foolish,

remind us that You are the One who speaks life
into barrenness.

Help us believe You're still writing the story,
even when it seems too late.

Like Joseph,
teach us to remain faithful when we're forgotten in
the dark.

When betrayal and injustice bury the dream,
give us a faith that outlasts resentment.

Form in us a resilient trust...
one that holds on, even in the pit, even in the
prison.

Like Hannah,
teach us to pray when we feel forgotten by You.

When our longings ache and our prayers echo
back in silence,
receive our tears as worship.

Remind us that lament is not a lack of faith,
but often its purest expression.

Like David,
teach us to be patient when anointing doesn't
mean arrival.
When we've been called but not yet released,
when we know who we are but must still wait to
step into it,
guard us from shortcuts.
Form humility, integrity, and readiness in the caves
and hidden places.

Like Mary,
teach us to say yes when the promise disrupts the
present.
When obedience costs us our comfort and clarity,
let wonder rise where fear wants to take hold.
Give us the courage to carry what we don't fully
understand.

Like the disciples,

teach us to stay still when the Spirit says wait.

When we'd rather move or build or fix,

help us remain until power comes from on high.

Let our stillness become surrender.

Let our waiting become formation.

God, You waste nothing.

Not the delays.

Not the detours.

Not the days when nothing seems to be

happening.

So make us people of the long road…

anchored in promise,

formed by patience,

alive to Your presence.

Teach us to wait well.

And let it be holy.

Amen.

Appendix: Companion Guide for Reflection, Prayer, and Group Use

For Individuals, Groups, or Communities in the Middle of the Wait

These questions are intended to accompany you long after the final page. They can be used week by week, or as a retreat-style reflection. Take your time. Don't rush resolution. The goal is not to find quick answers but to remain open to what the Spirit is revealing as you wait.

1. Naming the Wait

- Where in your life are you currently experiencing delay, silence, or uncertainty?
- What emotions are most present in your waiting—frustration, fear, numbness, hope?

- How have your expectations of God shifted as a result?

2. Looking Back

- Think of a past season of waiting. What did you learn? What did you lose? What did God reveal?
- What false beliefs about timing, worth, or God's faithfulness did that season expose?
- How did that wait shape your prayer life, or your view of Scripture?

3. Hearing the Stories Anew

- Which character's journey resonated with you the most—Abraham and Sarah, Joseph, Hannah, David, Mary, or the disciples? Why?

- Did any particular moment in their story disrupt your assumptions about what faith "should" look like?

- What do these stories teach you about the difference between delay and denial?

4. Honest Prayer

- What are the prayers you haven't been able to say aloud?

- Where have you felt like God was absent or unresponsive? What do you need in that place?

- If you could write one line of Scripture to describe your current posture, what would it be?

5. Trusting in Formation, Not Just Fulfillment

- How is waiting shaping your character—not just your circumstances?
- Where do you feel the Spirit inviting you to let go of control?
- What might it look like to live as if formation is the goal, even if the outcome never changes?

6. With Others

- Who do you know that is also waiting? What would it mean to walk with them instead of rushing them?
- What stories of delayed hope or slow miracles could you share with someone else?

- What kind of community do you need in this season? How can you help create it for others?

A Final Prompt

Take time to write your own story of waiting. Not the version tied with a bow, but the honest version. Start with where you are. Don't skip the ache. Don't rush the ending. Offer it to God.

Reflection Notes

Use this space to reflect on what God is stirring in

you…

A Letter to Fellow Waiters

Dear fellow waiter,

If you've made it to the end of this book, I want to pause and say this to you directly: I'm proud of you. Not because you have it all figured out, but because you've chosen to linger in the tension. You didn't skip to the end. You stayed with the ache. You let yourself read about others who waited in confusion and contradiction and allowed their stories to meet you in your own.

Waiting can feel like wasted time. It can feel like punishment or delay or some cosmic test of your patience. But I hope these pages have shown you that waiting can also be the place where God does His deepest work. Not after everything is resolved. Not when clarity comes. But right in the middle of the mess.

You don't have to love this season. You don't have to fake peace when your heart feels frayed. But you are allowed to believe that God is still present. Still good. Still forming you in ways that may not be obvious yet.

If you find yourself returning to these stories again later, I hope you notice things you missed the first time. If you find yourself in a small group or a quiet room, reflecting on your own waiting, I hope you know you're not alone. There are others—like you—holding on. Praying through silence. Laughing in disbelief. And trusting, even if only by a thread.

Keep showing up. Even when it's quiet.

And remember: God is not only found in the answers, but in the asking.

With you in the waiting,

Macho

Connect with Macho

You can find more of Macho's writing, reflections, and upcoming projects at **macholara.com** There you'll find links to his blog, recent sermons, social media accounts, and resources for churches and small groups.

BONUS

Teaser: Ctrl+Alt→Believe

The following excerpt is from the introduction and epilogue of my next book, set to release in 2006. If *Those Who Wait* met you in the middle of silence, this next book will walk with you through the rebuilding.

Ctrl+Alt→Believe *INTRODUCTION*

What do you do when faith stops working?

Maybe you've prayed, read, worshiped, served, but the clarity you once had is gone. Maybe faith feels fragile now, like something you're barely holding onto. Maybe you've lost trust, lost hope, or lost the ability to believe like you once did.

If that's where you are, this book is for you.

Not to give you easy answers.

Not to rush you back to certainty. But to walk with you through the questions, the doubts, the losses, and the shifts that come when faith changes.

Because faith was never meant to stay the same.

It was always meant to grow.

Sometimes, though, growth doesn't look like what we imagined. It begins with unraveling. With grief. With surrender. And often, before anything can be rebuilt, something has to be let go. Something has to be… deleted.

Not in anger.

Not in defeat.

But with trust. With honesty. With the courage to admit that what once worked no longer does.

That's the moment we tend to resist. We want to skip ahead to resurrection, to restoration, to the parts where things make sense again. But real transformation rarely begins with clarity. It begins with a crash. And sometimes, the reboot we need isn't about getting back to normal but about letting go of what *was* so we can make space for what *could* be.

You don't have to read this book in order. If you're in the middle of loss, start at Chapter 2.

If you're wrestling with doubt, go straight to Chapter 3.
If you're just trying to figure out what life looks like after the unraveling, jump ahead to Chapter 10.

This isn't a program. It's a conversation. An invitation.
A space to breathe, to ask hard questions, and to

believe, even if only barely, that God meets us in the unraveling.

So take a deep breath.
You don't need to fix anything right now.
You don't need to pretend everything's okay.

Just start where you are.

Ctrl+Alt→Believe *PROLOGUE*

I didn't see it coming.

That's the part that still unsettles me. There was no dramatic moment, no clear sign that my life was about to change. Just a slow unraveling. small symptoms I brushed off until they refused to be ignored. Until they forced me to pay attention. Until I found myself staring at a screen, reading words that hinted at a reality I wasn't prepared for.

Multiple sclerosis.

I had spent my life troubleshooting problems, analyzing errors, and finding solutions. But this wasn't a system I could reboot. There was no way to predict what would come next.

And that terrified me.

I'd like to say I responded with unwavering faith, that I immediately turned to God and found peace. But that wouldn't be the truth.

The truth is, I wrestled.

I wrestled with fear. With doubt. With the aching question that sat heavy in my chest: Why?

I had believed that faith meant figuring things out. finding the lesson, making sense of the suffering, trusting that if I did the right things, things would work out. But this? This wasn't something I could fix.

So what happens when faith isn't about fixing? When trusting God isn't about holding things together, but about releasing them?

I used to think surrender meant defeat. But maybe surrender is something else entirely.

Maybe letting go isn't about quitting. Maybe it's about finally admitting that I was never in control to begin with.

This book isn't about answers. It's about the moment you realize you don't have them. It's about what happens when life doesn't go according to plan. when faith feels fragile, when trust feels impossible, when control slips through your fingers and all that's left is a choice:

Will you fight to hold on, or will you learn to let go?

I didn't know the answer yet. But my body was about to force the question.